MW01168590

Gus Will Stop

By Ann Witkowski

Illustrated by Robin Boyer

Target Skill Review

Scott Foresman
is an imprint of

PEARSON

Where will Gus stop?
Gus will stop to get Dot.

Gus will stop.

Dot will hop in.

Where will Gus stop next?

Gus will stop to get Ted and Fred.

Gus will stop.

Ted and Fred will jump in.

Where will Gus stop next?
Gus will stop to get Rin.

Gus will stop.

Come on, Rin. Get in.

Gus will stop at the last stop.

Have fun, Dot, Ted, Fred, and Rin.